10 Little Rules for Sharing Your Story

by
Frank Winters

Copyright ©2024 by Frank Winters
All rights reserved.

ISBN: 979-8-9901971-7-6

Published by Little Rules Publishing

The original illustrations in this book
were created by the talented
Nate Tys
@thesnazzychameleon

DEDICATION

I dedicate this little book to my recently deceased parents, Jan and Frank Winters. At the time of this writing, my father has been gone for just over a year, and my mother for about two months. Their passing prompted thoughts of their legacy. Those thoughts brought me to contemplation of what I can and should do to honor them and all they have instilled in me. Both my mom and dad were life-long learners, teachers, and servants. This world is populated by both passengers and crew members. Passengers are along for the ride while crew members take pride in making sure everything they are connected with works as well as it can. Both Jan and Frank were consummate crew members.

My father was a natural storyteller. Around the dinner table, Dad would tell us in detail about his day at the offices of New York Telephone. He managed his team with unwavering philosophical principles. The one that sticks in my mind the strongest is, "The people come first." To this day I can hear those words in his voice. In those days, job openings in his industry were advertised in monthly professional trade journals. When Dad found an opening that might advance the career of one of his reports, he would circle it and leave it on that employee's desk. This kind action was often met with some confusion over his intent. I remember one of his reports asking, "Are you trying to get rid of me?" Dad's answer was concise and consistent: "The people come first." Many of the strongest members of his teams moved on to other positions, but my dad asserted that he never truly lost anyone.

Although this was not his primary intention, he added those people to his network of trusted colleagues throughout his industry. Dad's unit gained a reputation as a springboard for career advancement. Also not Dad's initial intention, but he wound up with many of the company's future shakers and movers vying for the openings on his team. By putting the people first, Dad had a positive impact on New York Telephone, his slice of the industry and, most importantly, the people on his team. Growing up, I thought that every kid at 14 or 15 got exposure to those kinds of stories. It wasn't until I was well underway in my own career did I understand those stories were Dad's unique gift.

My mother had her own style for instilling virtues. As a family of six, we did not have much extra money. Family vacations (sometimes only a weekend long) typically took the form of camping trips. I thought hotel rooms and restaurants were cool, but hanging out in the woods was so much more fun. Camping was full of rituals for the Winters; singing around the campfire, my father cooking bacon or Spam with eggs on the Coleman stove, the handmade wooden campsite sign with all our names on it, and an American flag on the dining fly that covered the picnic table – car camping at its best for sure.

The most meaningful ritual happened under my mom's direction. In her kind and loving way, Mom insisted we leave the campsite better than we found it. She also insisted we leave a courtesy pile of firewood for the next campers. She would tell us a different story each time about the next family to use the site. These stories included names and details about their adventure. One that sticks out goes like this: The family had car trouble along the way and got to the site after dark. They had planned hotdogs over the fire for dinner. The kids were overtired and hungry. Our pile of wood got their trip off to a great start.

We came to expect and enjoy these simple rituals. We didn't know it at the time, but Mom was instilling a sense of stewardship and empathy in each of us for people we would never meet. Heck, the people in Mom's stories didn't even exist.

Mom's mantra to leave the campsite better than we found it led me to a new North Star to guide my life. In the weeks following her death, I realized that not only do I need to leave the campsite better, I need to leave the *world* better by my actions in it. This book is one of my attempts to maximize my positive impact on the world.

I believe there are people (maybe yourself) thinking great thoughts and doing great things, but the impact of those thoughts and deeds might be limited by an unwillingness to share those stories, or less than ideal communication strategies. If you make small, meaningful changes in your storytelling as a result of this book, you will be helping me live out my mother's legacy. For that I am grateful.

ACKNOWLEDGMENTS

Michael Gervais, even though we have not met in person, you feel like a friend to me. On every long solo car ride you and your Finding Mastery podcast guests are in my ears. Thank you for helping create the internal mindset so necessary for me to have undertaken this project. Thank you also for reviewing a draft of this book, and for your direct encouragement. That felt like I had dipped a toe in the big leagues. It felt good and it felt right. As I type these acknowledgements, your words "No one does it alone" ring loud in my ears, so with that – on with the gratitude.

Next I need to acknowledge you, the reader. Without your willingness to pick up this book and have a look, this would have been of limited value. You are the one who will leave the world a better place with your stories.

Chilling (literally) in a rocky stream in northern Vermont after a long day of coaching a youth mountain bike race camp, I had a wonderful conversation about this book and about you, the future reader, with my dear friend Angel Vides. Coach Angel, I vividly remember your first comment when I talked about what I was working on. In your fiery El Salvadorian voice you said "Dude, you are going to help so many people with this." For that, and the rest of your thoughtful questions and comments, I am grateful.

My dear friend Christine Kendal, you helped me through some times that would have been darker without our long conversations. You believed in me, and kept me writing.

Nate Tys, it feels like just yesterday that I was helping teach you to ski as a little kid. Now, here you are, a professional artist. I was so impressed how, after one hour discussing the book, you captured its spirit through your illustrations. The publishing team and I incorporated the first draft of each of your drawings without edit.

Wendy Price, your eagle eye on my many typos was only the beginning. I appreciate your candor in pointing out the parts of the book that didn't flow, or didn't make much sense. You took the worst parts of my writing and guided me to make them some of the best parts.

Finally, I want to express my gratitude to you, Carol Pearson. You are not only a loving sister, but also a true friend, and a mentor. You are helping not only me, but the thousands of people touched by the 10 Little Rules books to live out our mother's legacy – to leave the world better than we found it. Empowering readers to intentionally create and live by their own rules is the kind of impact that scales. The ripples from the pebble you tossed in the water will just keep going. You are courage personified.

Frank Winters

FOREWORD

It is my great honor to introduce the world to this book, written by a smart, talented and soulful man who also happens to be my kid brother. Frank's commitment to this project, to sharing his story in his own way, has been a joy to witness. His quest to learn from everything he experiences and everyone he meets is remarkable. I'm a better person for having him in my life.

And now Frank is part of this 10 Little Rules Community. He's expanded our vision of what 10 Little Rules can be, and for that I am ever grateful.

My hope as you read this book? That you learn to cherish your own powerful story and know how desperately the world needs to hear those authentic storytellers who can make things better just by being heard.

See you around the campfire. I'll bring the s'mores.

Carol Pearson
Frank's sister & founder of 10 Little Rules

Frank Winters

10 Little Rules for Sharing Your Story

CONTENTS

Introduction 19

Rule 1 — Share Your Story 25

Rule 2 — Invite Others In 49

Rule 3 — Be Scared 59

Rule 4 — Read the Room..75

Rule 5 — Compliment Your Listeners 89

Rule 6 — Think Beyond the Elevator Pitch 99

Rule 7 — Understand Your Brain 111

Rule 8 — Do Something Harder 133

Rule 9 — Play the Pause 147

Rule 10 — Embrace the Joy 159

Your Turn, Your Rules 172

Frank Winters

INTRODUCTION

When I first talked to my sister Carol Pearson, founder of 10 Little Rules, about writing this book, I had a different title in mind. As with any book in this *10 Little Rules* series, the title really matters. It matters because, unlike the title of most books, it sets the structure for the entire book. I had *10 Little Rules for Public Speaking* in mind; then Carol and I talked and she challenged me to broaden the intent and purpose.

For most of us, the amount of time in our lives we are actually speaking in public is small. For some people that amount of time is zero. Yet the opportunities we have to share our stories are nearly limitless. Any time we spend practicing compelling, meaningful, purpose-driven communication can have big impacts. I have found that the rules I put together for sharing my stories worked their way into many aspects of my life, far beyond the time I spend at the podium. Although I am not (yet) a YouTuber, the difference between those who make it big and those equally skilled in their craft who have limited audiences, lies in the way they share their stories. I thank Carol for expanding the reach of this book, but more importantly for helping me apply what I have developed in public speaking to the benefit of other areas of my life ... and hopefully yours. Whether you find yourself standing at the front of the room to speak or not, I hope you develop your own set of rules for sharing your story. And I hope your stories shine through in a way that leaves the world a better place.

Let's start by taking some pressure off. You don't need to apply all 10 of my rules to have success. In fact, you really don't need to apply any of them. I hope to expose enough of my thought process so you can develop your own rules. Maybe some of my rules will resonate with you. If you want to use some or all of mine, knock your socks off. Hopefully the process of defining your own rules will let them really become part of you.

To get started, just deploy the one or two rules or practices that feel like they might work for you. As you do, watch and listen for the reaction. I expect you will feel some energy coming back to you. When you do, embrace it. Lean into it. You probably hear people talk about the importance of living in the moment. I am most present, with the biggest portion of my brain firing, when I am sharing a story. For me, the bigger the audience, and the more important the story, the higher the likelihood that I will get to a flow state. You've probably heard of athletes reaching a flow state when an extreme challenge meets a heightened skill level, and they are in "the zone." It's happened to me a few times while skiing, canoe racing or mountain biking. I reach that same state of consciousness much more frequently engaged in public speaking.

It's hard to describe, but it only happens when I am performing well, and in a situation *outside* my comfort zone. When it happens, there is a thrill and a high that lingers. Writing this book, I took a look back at some of these peak moments and attempted to pull apart the setup and actions that got me there. This reflection, along with lots of listening to others, formed the basis for my 10 rules.

The principles I use to prepare for a big speech work equally well for an important phone call, a conversation at the office, or even a good talk with my kids. Keeping your rules in mind will make you a better communicator, consciously and even subconsciously. Your dinner table conversations could have the same kind of impact on a loved one's future as my father's stories about his work and his philosophies had on mine.

This book is filled with thoughts and ideas, some of which might be original. Some have been rattling around in my head for years; others are relatively new. Some came from the conversations posted in Dr. Michael Gervais's Finding Mastery podcast series (https://findingmastery.com/podcasts). You'll notice I refer to Dr. Mike often in this book. If anyone recognizes any of the other ideas and wants to give credit to the originator, please let me know.

You might be thinking about your own confidence level right now and wondering if you should continue reading. Truth is, your confidence level is sort of irrelevant. What matters is whether your confidence is rising or falling. The simple act of sitting down and starting to write this little book has boosted my self-confidence. As a coach of a youth mountain bike race team, I ask my riders where confidence comes from. I get a lot of great answers, and a few blank stares. These are a bunch of hard working, ambitious middle-schoolers and high-schoolers. I propose to them that confidence in this case does *not* come from affirmation from your coach or your parents. It does *not* come from your times on a score sheet. It does *not* come from the medal ceremony on the podium. Confidence comes from the promises you keep to yourself, and the stories you tell yourself.

Thank you for picking up this book and reading this far. You are the most important part of this promise I made to myself. If anything in this book or our conversations that follow help you, I have honored my parent's legacy by leaving the world just a bit better.

Let's jump in. Each of the 10 chapters is titled with one of my rules, and ends with some questions to help you dive deeper, and space to explore your own.

Frank Winters

RULE 1
Share Your Story

Humans have occupied Earth for about 300,000 years.

The wheel was invented about 7,000 years ago.

Based on this, only two percent of human existence has happened since the wheel. Only three tenths of a percent of our existence has occurred since the first Crusades. Three hundredths of a percent of our time has been since the first computer. Modern life as we know it is a drop in the bucket of our collective humanity.

Let's start way back in time, with the things that are innately human. The rate of change in our technology and social norms has far outstripped our biological evolution. These days there seems to be an inverse relationship between how connected we are and how well we understand each other. The more we are technologically connected, the less we know about each other as humans. Yet it's the things that resonate deep in our beings that line up with our DNA. These are the things that are innately human.

Extreme skier Glen Plake might have thought he was just saying something silly while sitting by a campfire high in the Sierras on an overnight summertime backcountry ski trip. He said, "At times like these, it's important to remember there have always been times like these."

Glen nailed it. Sitting around a fire telling stories is something humans have been doing throughout our existence. I believe good storytelling has a profound impact on us because it is wired deep in our souls.

It's worth looking at how our prehistoric ancestors worked together and communicated as we dive into what it really means to share our stories.

Share your story. Let's take this rule one word at a time, starting with "share." When you share something, there is a two-way exchange. A shared experience, like a meal or a campfire, typically has the most impact in person – so it seems a bit ironic to me that you are reading this and I am writing this. I am about to tell you that the act of sharing your story in person, using tools humans have had since the beginning, is the first part of my first rule.

In his book "Knowing What We Know," Simon Winchester explains that the first evidence of writing dates back about five thousand years (Winchester, 2023). This is only about one and a half percent of the time humans have been around. In defense of the written word, Winchester goes on to explain how the written word radically transformed communication. Once written languages evolved independently in different parts of the world at roughly the same time, humans could scale the audience for their knowledge. They could reach those who they would never have the opportunity to interact with personally. Technological advancements, from the printing press to the internet, continue to further scale the potential audience of the written word. Yet even with all that, I still maintain the most impactful communications happen in person.

Sharing a story goes far beyond the verbal. It starts with the eyes and includes the whole body. Winchester asserts that before the written word, all information (including that which would help us survive) was passed on through stories, poetry, performance, songs, dances, games and rituals. Clearly what we learned in grammar school about the prehistoric period of oral traditions employed far more than simply words.

Today, there are some fantastic story tellers who cannot hear or speak. The strength of their sign language and the feelings they convey through using their body is amazing. Sharing our story starts with what we are going to say, but quickly moves into how we are going to say it, and how we are going to make it shine using those physical elements that just are not possible via a text. Don't worry; it's not about acting. All you need to do is be fully present and fully genuine and your story will shine through. It also helps if you get out from behind the podium so people can see you.

A participant in a public speaking seminar I presented asked, "How do you avoid reading your talk?" My answer was simple: "I don't write it." Instead, I practice sharing my story.

Now, I recognize that's how my mind works, and you likely have strengths I don't. I struggled with reading and writing as a child. Poor spelling is still an embarrassment. I grew up with undiagnosed dyslexia. That is by no means an excuse; my disability created other abilities. We all build on our strengths to compensate for or mitigate a weakness. Certainly our brains have much in common, but they each work a little differently. If writing your story helps you organize your thoughts so you can better tell your story, great. Do that. Then, when the prep work is over and it's time to share your story, I would challenge you to practice that story with minimal notes, or even just a few pictures, to organize your flow.

If we were at a party, and you started sharing your story with me, you wouldn't pull it out of your pocket or fire up your laptop. You'd choose a more natural approach to connect.

Sometimes we think that in formal settings our stories need to be perfect. I am planning to go through many edit passes on this book to polish it up. When I am sharing my story in person, I don't worry about the polish. I just fall back on my preparation and let it rip. *Don't let the perfect be the enemy of the good.* I will take a genuine unpolished story that is told with conviction and passion over a perfectly polished robotic presentation any day.

Share **your** story. The next word I want to highlight is "your." The word "unique" is often misused. Most times when we say unique, we really mean rare. A football announcer talks about the unique speed of a wide receiver. But is his speed really unique? Does he have a world record in the 40 meter dash? You, however, are truly unique. There is no other person in the world with your combined set of experiences and thoughts. The word "unique" also brings to mind words like "special" or "precious". One-of-a-kind items have great value and are well cared for. Embrace the fact that what makes you truly unique also makes your stories unique. Be yourself. When facing an audience, either on stage in a big room or face to face with one person, remember that you have thoughts and perspectives they don't. Remember also, that everyone you encounter knows something you don't. (We'll talk more about that when we get to Rule 2 – Invite Others In.

Your stories don't need to be about you. You might share a story in your industry or for a volunteer organization. What makes those stories unique is that it's you sharing them using your unique set of experiences and perspectives.

Now, let's talk about sharing your **story**. This takes us back to the beginning of this chapter. Stories are innately human. Our DNA has evolved around stories, so our ability to understand and act on what we hear in stories is in our biology, not just our psychology. Throughout most of the time humans have been on the earth, the primary mechanism for conveying information, for teaching and learning, has been through stories. Offspring of those who were adept storytellers survived at a higher rate (Kluger, 2017). Likewise, those who were better at listening to and learning from stories had a higher chance of survival. It was through stories that humans learned from the experience of others how to gather food, work together, share resources and outwit predators. A basic tenant of evolution is: those who survive pass on the genetic traits and consequently we strengthen our species.

You may have heard the term "the arc of a story." I like this term. It allows me to visualize the shape of the story. We start by building a foundation on which the shape will stand. This foundation is sometimes called the *exposition*. In the exposition we introduce characters, and may describe the setting. These are the places and conditions that exist before anything happens. The exposition can be brief and covers the contextual information important to our listener's understanding. Don't dwell on it. Details about the conditions and the characters can be included along the arc.

The arc begins to take shape and lift off the foundation as soon as we describe something meaningful that happens to one or more of the characters. This is called *rising action*. In many of the best stories, the events that happen build in the form of conflict. In this part of the story we reveal the motives of the characters in the way we describe their actions.

The peak of the arc is the *climax*. All of the happenings we describe in the rising action bring us to an outcome. The conflicts are resolved. Everything that happens as a result of the conflict is called *falling action*. These actions create the *resolution*, which describes the new state of the characters in their changed setting.

Note, as shown in the image on the next page, the resolution is higher than the exposition. That's because a well crafted story leaves the listener in a different place, perhaps more enlightened, challenged, or motivated.

Not all of your stories need to include all of these parts, but the idea is helpful to keep in mind. I'm a career geographer. Knowing that, you might think the most important part of the story to me is the geographic setting in the exposition. Not so. The parts of the story I focus on are the characters and their motives. In my opinion, a deep understanding of *who* is taking action and *why* is what makes a story compelling. Listeners of a truly compelling story are motivated to do something different as a result.

Skiing has been a passion of mine since I first learned as a high-school aged Boy Scout. My biggest ski hero is Hilaree Nelson; partly because of her skiing, partly because of the places she had the courage and skill to go to, and partly because of her thoughtfulness.

10 Little Rules for Sharing Your Story

In 2018, Rich Roll interviewed Hilaree Nelson. He re-released that interview in 2022 on YouTube after Hilaree's tragic death in the Himalayas (Roll, 2022). In that interview, Hilaree discussed the lack of female role models in the field of exploration. This speaks volumes about Hilaree. The incredible effort she put into climbing and skiing goes far beyond her own accomplishments. She did those things (in part at least) in service of others.

It's apparent that a big part of Hilaree's service to others was encouraging women to express their greatness in domains dominated by men. She suggested that women are often more compelling story tellers because of the tendency a woman has to dive deeper into *why* the story matters, rather than focusing on what happened. So it's not the stories themselves that are compelling; it's the way in which those stories are told.

Using Hilaree's example, we can carefully craft our own stories so our listeners see themselves in our words. If we look at the way Hilaree works the arc of her story, it's not just about the climbs, the tactics, the cool equipment or the physical challenges she met. Her rising action includes philosophical discussions of what these things mean in a broader life context. The conflict she describes is not just about the bitter cold, or the exhaustion. Her conflicts emphasize her internal struggle around the impact of her career on her family, and what it feels like to be thousands of miles from home with little to no way to communicate.

Hilaree shaped her stories in a way that had a powerful impact. First, they encouraged women to be boldly present in *any* field, despite existing gender expectations. Second, she encouraged us all to express the deeper meaning in what we are doing, going beyond the *who* and *what* and digging deeply into the *why*. Finally, her stories enlighten some of the struggles many of us face, serving as guideposts for those who might follow.

We don't have to follow in Hilaree's actual footsteps of big mountain climbing to learn from her example. With our own thoughts expanded by considering the challenges, triumphs and tragedies in Hilaree's stories, we can become a little more intentional in how we choose to live, and the way we choose to tell our stories.

Maybe you and I will have a chance to share our stories together in person someday.

your turn...

Take a few minutes now to explore your thoughts about sharing your own story.

First, what does it mean to **share** your story? Think back to a great conversation you've had.

Was it over email or text? Was it face to face? What was the setting? Did you tell any stories?

Use a page or two to write about it on the following journaling pages.

Now picture recreating that feeling. Take what you accomplished during that great conversation and transfer that feeling to a story you are planning to tell or would like to tell. There are no bad ideas here. What can you do to recreate that great conversation with different audiences over and over again? Start small and leave a page or two to scale up as you refine your rules.

Share *your* story.

Your stories will be unique because *you* are unique.

On another journal page, list two interests, skills or experiences in your life that seem extremely different from one and other. List one on the left and one on the right. Now list two more pairs, and two more. Write down ideas for using a story from one side of your list while talking about something on the other side.

Share your ***story***.

Think back to that wonderful conversation you remembered. Keeping the idea of the story arc in mind, break out the exposition. Use a few more of your journaling pages.

Who were the characters?
What place, conditions, smells, other sensory inputs do you remember?

Can you think of rising action in that conversation? Climax? Falling action?
What was the motive – why did that matter?

If you have forgotten the details, or not noticed them at the time, that's OK. It's fine to make up some details to fill in the gaps. This will make your thoughts about that conversation even better.

Frank Winters

10 Little Rules for Sharing Your Story

Frank Winters

10 Little Rules for Sharing Your Story

Frank Winters

10 Little Rules for Sharing Your Story

Frank Winters

10 Little Rules for Sharing Your Story

10 Little Rules for Sharing Your Story

Frank Winters

RULE 2
Invite Others In

As we talked about in Rule 1, everyone you encounter knows something you don't. When we invite others in to shape our stories, the process of storytelling becomes an opportunity for learning. Whether your audience is one or one thousand, inviting them in is an important part of keeping them engaged. We learn best from people who are engaged with us. Bonus: Genuinely inviting others to shape our stories is also a sure-fire way to avoid projecting arrogance.

The current overdose of 24-hour media, with its constant barrage of divisive politics, have left many among us with a sense of certainty of our own views. Many have become dead certain that "their" side is absolutely right and the other is absolutely wrong. In this mindset, a contrary view now becomes a threat.

On a physical level, threats are processed in the amygdala or brain stem – far from where creative thoughts can happen (more on this in Rule 7). And as the old quote (accredited to Mark Twain but still a matter of debate) goes:

"It ain't what you don't know that gets you into trouble. It's what you know for sure that just ain't so."

Instead of starting from a position of certainty, let's deliberately start with a spirit of curiosity. As a manager, I've told my team that the opinions most useful for me are those that differ from my current thoughts. Inviting others to shape our stories allows our stories to grow. Your stories also engage the audience in a non-threatening way, meaning the information the listeners are taking in will be processed in the creative part of their brain, rather than being seen as a threat.

10 Little Rules for Sharing Your Story

While I was writing this chapter, I gave a presentation at the National States Geographic Information Council's (NSGIC) annual meeting. In my opening I said: "I approach this conversation not with certainty, but with curiosity."

After I had made my points I asked the audience: "Who has the first comment? Who has a different way to look at this? Has a dissenting view? OK, who has the first question?"

The audience was far more engaged than if I had just flipped to a slide with a big question mark on it and asked, "Are there any questions?" The first comment was in the form of a question, and a really good discussion followed that organically flowed over into the breaks.

This kind of engagement carries over into our personal lives too. My son Luke was over last night, and we dove into map data together. He proposed a plan to climb and ski a seldom skied area on a group of fairly remote mountains in Maine called the Crockers. One possible approach would start at the top of Sugarloaf ski area, follow the Appalachian Trail 2,000 vertical feet down, hit the valley, then climb 2,000 vertical feet to a campsite near the base of the zone. From there, we would switch from alpine touring skis to ice axes and crampons. We would dig test pits to check the stability of the snowpack and, if safe, climb and ski the steep slide paths. The beginning of a plan included an early start, lots of specialty gear, lots of water and food. The route has several egress options, each of which would take a while. While we were both confident in our ability to get in and out of that zone safely, and we were finding out all we could about it, the thing that had me so excited was *what we didn't know*. We were filled with curiosity. We might not ever attempt it, and if we do there is a good chance that we turn back without skiing it. All the while, we are stoked by curiosity.

your turn...

Invite others in

How can you develop your skill at inviting others to shape your stories?

Do you remember a time you were genuinely curious?
How did that feel?
Did you ask questions?
How were your questions received?
Did you connect with the person you were talking with?

Use the following blank journal pages to reflect and record your ideas.

Frank Winters

10 Little Rules for Sharing Your Story

10 Little Rules for Sharing Your Story

Frank Winters

RULE 3
Be Scared

Comedian Jerry Seinfeld cites a clinical study that found the number one fear in America is public speaking. Number two is death. He quipped that Americans at a funeral would rather be in the box than giving the eulogy.

Where does this fear come from? In his book "The First Rule of Mastery: Stop Worrying about What Other People Think of You," Dr. Mike explains that the fear of other people's opinions (FOPO) is deeply rooted in our DNA and is often maladaptive, while being a constrictor of human performance (Gervais, 2023).

Throughout most of my life, I tried hard to avoid emotions like grief, anger or sadness – what I thought of as negative emotions because they made me uncomfortable. Eventually I realized my efforts to suppress or avoid these emotions prevented me from being fully present in the moment, and prevented me from fully connecting with others.

Eventually I learned that emotions and feelings are not at all the same thing. Emotions are observable physical reactions to stimuli, including thoughts. Emotions are visceral, physical reactions. They are automatic – meaning we have no control over them – and they are temporary. Our feelings, on the other hand, come from the mind's subjective processing and reactions to those emotions. We have little to no control over the emotion, while we can process it and change the experience of our feelings with conscious thought.

At this point in my life, I am often surprised by my own emotional reactions to things. First of all, I have become much more tolerant of the "discomfort" of emotional reactions. Further, I am open to embracing and feeling the full range of human emotions. When I am surprised by my emotions, I can be confident that I am not artificially manipulating my feelings or suppressing them. My emotions and feelings are neither right nor wrong; they naturally co-exist. It's kind of a relief to allow myself to truly embrace raw emotions and consciously consider how I feel.

Let me share a personal example. In November 2020, I spent a week in a hotel with my sisters and their families following the death of our father. The hotel had kitchens in every room, so my sister-in-law came up with the idea of cooking our own "hotel Thanksgiving." The night before the funeral, we were all just crazy enough to pull it off and we had a memorable meal with the extended family. I made a little toast at that gathering and explained that, once again, I was surprised by my own feelings and explained that in that moment, I felt gratitude. I was grateful for a remarkable week reconnecting with my sisters, for all the nieces and nephews, for the examples and stories my father had shared over the years – for so many things. I gave myself a pass on the thought that this was a time I was supposed to be mournful. I encouraged everyone to just feel how they felt.

It became clear to me that week that I can have different, seemingly contrasting, feelings at the same time. In this case I was experiencing grief and gratitude simultaneously, and that was OK. The fact that you might experience fear while sharing your story (or at least leading up to it) need not preclude other feelings like gratitude for the opportunity or enthusiasm for the topic.

When preparing to share a story, I often feel some fear. I have become totally fine with that. There are different kinds of fear, and fear can be super useful. When we are in a truly dangerous situation it's the fear response that can give us the best chance to escape unharmed. If we let ourselves become a little more comfortable with fear, we are less likely to freeze in those truly threatening situations.

Hopefully while storytelling we are not in a situation that can cause bodily harm; that would signify some profoundly bad storytelling. The fear we experience in sharing our story is nevertheless real. Fear of embarrassment is super powerful. Even though rationally we understand we are physically safe, we might be well outside our comfort zone. Allow yourself to experience that emotion.

The first step to controlling yourself while experiencing fear is to name it. Notice I didn't say "control your fear." I said "control yourself" while experiencing your fear. As it happens, Name Your Fears is Rule 6 in Carol Pearson's book, "10 Little Rules for a Blissy Life" (Pearson, 2016). (I had not remembered that when I was writing the outline for this book; but the idea has relevance to so many of us on our particular journeys.)

The act of naming your fear physically moves the thoughts from the primitive part of our brain to the more advanced, rational and creative part of the brain. We can actually move fearful thoughts to a more productive part of our brains, and use them in a positive way.

10 Little Rules for Sharing Your Story

The time right before the start of a mountain bike race can be really trying for the racers on my youth team. Before the race I often ask a rider, "Are you nervous?" The answer, with a quiver in the voice, is almost always, "Yes." My response is almost always "Good!" I then thank the rider for being honest with me and, more importantly, with themselves. I explain that the act of saying you are nervous – naming your fear and allowing yourself to be scared – is the first step to controlling yourself and your reaction to that fear. I ask them to embrace the nerves, and tell them I feel really good they are nervous, because being nervous means this matters to them. My time as a coach is well-spent when I know the riders care.

I go on to explain that the neuro-chemical response their fear creates gives them everything they need for both mental and physical acuity and high performance. The key is to not let all that energy blow up like a Roman candle. Be scared, then control how you move forward.

When sharing your story, it's OK to tell your audience you are nervous. Just do it in a positive way. To put a positive spin on my admission of nerves, I've said things like, "Wow this is an impressive, kind of intimidating group, but let's press on together." Admitting your feelings makes you human, and therefore more relatable. Your audience might even be subconsciously rooting for you. In fact, anytime you expose your vulnerabilities to your audience, you make opportunities for deeper connections.

Sometimes when I am sharing a story there is a whole different narrative going on inside my head. Odd, random, and often unhelpful thoughts come into my mind. That can be very disconcerting. I have been on stage and the words coming out my mouth are entirely different from the thoughts in my mind. On more than one occasion I asked a trusted, honest friend how it went and explained some of what was going on inside my head. That question is always followed by a good laugh and a reassurance that the talk was fine and those thoughts never shone through.

These uncontrolled thoughts get to the root of why many people fear public speaking. What if thoughts I can't control throw me off my game and I freeze up? I will have humiliated myself in front of an audience. Over the years I have learned one powerful reality: Those thoughts are not mine unless I make them mine. Yes, those random thoughts are coming from my mind, but I am not consciously invoking them – and I have learned to actively dismiss them. A thought that does not serve me well gets recognized then quickly dismissed. With practice, that now happens quicker than I can say the words "hello" and "goodbye" to them.

Controlling our thoughts is a learnable skill that, like any skill, can be practiced. Meditation is a great place to start. There are many forms of meditation; one I practice regularly is called *concentrative meditation*, also referred to as *fixed attentiveness*.

In the morning after a good workout, inspired by Micki Beach and her book "10 Little Rules for Finding Your Truth" (Beach, 2020), I get into Child's Pose, close my eyes, and repeat this little mantra: "Is it loving? Is it helpful?" It doesn't really matter what the words of the mantra are. What matters is the act of directing my attention to just those words. Thoughts do enter my mind while I am repeating my mantra. I don't get upset by these thoughts; it's a completely normal part of meditation. I just dismiss them as quickly as I can. Over time, I have gotten really efficient at recognizing them and letting them go without judgment.

One morning, while meditating, I was distracted by the sounds of cars driving by. I quickly thought of how blessed I am to have this time to meditate while others are rushing off to work. I used the sound of each car as a trigger to think more deeply on my mantra. Within a handful of seconds, I no longer noticed the cars. This training of my mind has done wonders for the speed at which I can dismiss a thought that might not serve me well. It has given me a measure of awareness and control over my thoughts. While telling my stories, my mind is no longer subject to being hijacked by unhelpful thoughts.

Months after writing these last few paragraphs, I was delighted to hear Dr. Mark Leary (a renowned professor of psychology and neuroscience at Duke University) validate the insights I had drawn from my personal experiences on a podcast with Dr. Mike (https://findingmastery.com/podcasts/mark-leary/). When asked by Dr. Mike how to help people be more grounded and effective while speaking in public, Dr. Leary suggested a mindfulness practice to have some "control over our unruly brain," which tends to "think without our permission."

The training and techniques I am recommending here start with the reality that fear exists. When we recognize fear, name it, and then take measures to shape our relationship with it, fear no longer has complete control over us. We can begin to act with courage, understanding that courage cannot exist without fear. Some say that courage and fear are opposites. I say courage is a rational, deliberate response to proceed in the face of fear. Let's not confuse courage with recklessness, though. The distinction to me is that courage exists most often inside our safety zone, but outside our comfort zone. Recklessness is throwing caution to the wind with no consideration of safety.

Acting with courage – feeling the fear and knowing you can proceed in the face of it – feels good.

Frank Winters

your turn...

Be scared

Think of a time you were really scared. Now, think of a time you were really nervous.

Where in your body did you feel these emotions? Did both of those feelings create the same sensations in your body?

Now think of a time that you were scared or nervous, and carried on despite the fear. How did that make you feel?

Congratulate yourself in writing, using your own name. (Talking or writing to yourself in the third person has a profound physiological purpose. It activates the brain differently than our normal thoughts of ourselves, which can make our words more memorable.)

Frank Winters

10 Little Rules for Sharing Your Story

10 Little Rules for Sharing Your Story

RULE 4
Read the Room

My original thought for Rule 4 was Know Your Audience, then I changed it to Know your Participants. I changed it again to Read the Room.

This change came when I was on the selection committee for an influential job in a national not-for-profit. After one of the interviews, another member of the selection committee said, "I felt like I was in the audience, but I wanted to be in a conversation." The candidate put out a lot of the right well-rehearsed words, but did not leave room for any conversation. He neglected to read the room.

This idea dovetails with Rule 2 — Invite Others In. Inviting others to shape your story is one of the ways to move from having an audience to having participants. The participation can happen before, during and/or after the initial story depending on your style, comfort level and story content. The results will be the same: There will be more engagement.

Reading the room starts in advance of the conversation. It starts with understanding who you are talking with, what they are bringing to the conversation, and how they might be feeling. Let's think about how we can get to know the participants. When I prepare to give a talk at a conference, I often connect with the conference organizers and ask questions like:

- What is the makeup of the participants in terms of their careers, interests, and reason for attending?

- What problems are they collectively trying to solve?

- What do they have in common?

- What might they have in common with me?

- What are they sensitive to?

- How can I help them?

In some cases you might even have the opportunity to poll your participants before a session. The right questions can help target the story, and gives the participants agency and a sense of connection before the session even begins.

An adaptation of these same questions can create a meaningful mindset shift in preparing for a conversation with an individual.

Knowing the participant goes beyond figuring out what they might be thinking. I start by trying to think as they are thinking. Then I try to figure out what they might feel. Then I try to feel how they are feeling. This is something you don't need to get 100% right to be effective. That's actually a good thing, because it is impossible to predict what people are thinking and feeling. Just the act of trying to feel as they are will give you insights and allow you to speak with empathy.

In a 2024 editorial, NY Times reporters Aneesh Raman and Maria Flynn suggest that as artificial intelligence or AI takes on a portion of our tasks, humans should step up their activities in things that are innately human – like communication, collaboration, and empathy (Raman A. and Flynn, M., 2024).

We all want to be loved. When we are sharing a story, we want the participants to love that story. In turn we want them to love us. Performers long for the audience to love them. That's a scary thing, as are most things we long for but have little control over. Let's take control of that little dilemma right now. Pavarotti put it best when he said:

"Some singers want the audience to love them. I love the audience."

The word "love" has so many meanings and is even used as different parts of speech. The love we feel is a noun. In the Pavarotti quote, the word love is a verb. We actively put the audience first and give them something of value to them. Taking this approach will greatly increase the odds of your participants loving your story. And if they don't, who cares? You did your best in a selfless act. Love yourself for that. Celebrate it wildly.

Another way to think about this is to put your participants first, yourself second, and your supporting materials (slide deck) third.

Reading the room – and adapting your story accordingly – can be likened to the difference between a thermometer and a thermostat.

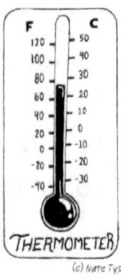

A thermometer takes the temperature of a room. That's its only job. A thermostat also takes the temperature of the room ... and then does something about it by making the necessary adjustments. Be a thermostat.

(c) Nate Tys

During a recent public speaking workshop, I was just about to start a somewhat technical topic, and I noticed the energy level was a little low. The sparks in some of the participants were not as bright as they had been. I knew the audience had been sitting for a while, so I told them we were about to cover something that might require a change in thinking. I asked them all to stand up with their arms at their sides. I then asked them to fold their arms. Then to put them back at their sides and shake them out. Then fold them again, but this time with the other arm on top. I asked them how they felt. Most said they were mildly uncomfortable. I then asked how many would have been able to tell me which hand you typically put on top. No one raised their hand.

The change I asked for was meaningless, yet there was a slight discomfort when I asked the group to make that change. In this case they experienced that discomfort even though they didn't even know they had a preference for which hand goes on top. That little exercise energized the room. It got them thinking about change. Also, crossing the centerline of our bodies with our appendages fires synapses across the right and left hemispheres of our brain. That has a tendency to reactivate parts of the brain that are sometimes temporarily dormant.

your turn...

Read the room

Go back to that great conversation we've been talking about, or think of another one.

What do you imagine the other person was thinking? What were they feeling? What sensation do you imagine they were feeling in their body?

Now think about a conversation you are planning, or one you would like to have. It could be one-on-one, in front of a big audience, or anything in between.

What can you do to read the room?
Who is the audience? What are they thinking?

What are they feeling? What can you say to make them feel better, more comfortable, more engaged? How can you set up your story in a way that invites them in and moves them from audience to willing participants?

Use the journaling pages that follow to record your thoughts and reflect on how you can read the room ... and even change the weather.

10 Little Rules for Sharing Your Story

10 Little Rules for Sharing Your Story

10 Little Rules for Sharing Your Story

Frank Winters

RULE 5
Compliment Your Listeners

I had the opportunity to give the keynote at the New York State Bridge Engineers conference. I started by saying, "I love engineers. My father was an engineer. My father would make a list of things to do around the house on a Saturday and when he finished something he would come into his office and cross it off the list with a straightedge. That is a fond memory of my father."

The participants in the audience got a kick out of that. Many saw themselves in that comment. That story might not have been as entertaining to a room full of poets or musicians. It worked because it was relevant to a characteristic shared by many in the room; and it rang true because it was sincere.

A natural next step after knowing your participants is to figure out what you like about them. If I can't come up with anything I like about the participants as a group, that means either I didn't do my homework or they should probably have another speaker.

I always welcome and encourage comments, challenges and questions from the participants. As I mentioned in Rule 2, I avoid asking, "Are there any questions?" Instead I ask: "Who has the first comment? Dissenting viewpoint? Questions?"

When someone speaks up, I ask them to introduce themselves. Then I compliment their comment or question, being careful to use their name. If I want the next comment or question, I better compliment the first one, and treat them with respect. It can be as simple as saying "That's a thoughtful question, Ellen."

Here's something you can try. Often before a presentation, I will quietly ask one of the participants to be a plant, and give them a question to ask if no one else does. When the question comes, I thank the plant by name for the good question and we are off and running. The act of having a planted questioner does something for both the participants and for me. It (often subconsciously) makes the participants more comfortable, and deactivates the part of the brain that processes threats. For me, I feel better having a partner who has agreed to help me. We are in on a fun little trick together. When the questions are over, I come clean and thank the plant for playing along. This brings us back to what Pavarotti said about loving the audience. It's all about them and what will leave them better.

When I don't know the answer to a question, I put it out to the audience to see what perspectives others have. Sometimes I offer to find out the answer or who to connect with so we can continue the conversation later. An interesting thing happens when telling a story in this way. I am freed from the pressure of being the expert. That freedom is one of the things that opens parts of my brain in the moment that otherwise lay dormant.

Sometimes, I catch myself saying internally, "Damn boy, that was good. I could never have come up with that sitting alone at my computer. I hope someone wrote that down because you might never hear that one again." We'll talk more about this idea in Rule 7.

your turn...

Compliment your listeners

Let's continue thinking about those participants you were just writing about in Rule 4.

What do you like about them?

What makes them special and unique, collectively and individually?

What lights you up about speaking to them?

10 Little Rules for Sharing Your Story

Frank Winters

10 Little Rules for Sharing Your Story

RULE 6
Think Beyond the Elevator Pitch

To take your impact to the next level, create 15-second, two-minute and 20-minute versions of your stories.

As humans, we have been blessed with many gifts. I believe the most important gift we have been given is time. Baseball is *America's pastime*. What? Why would I want time to pass? I want to revel in it. I love baseball. Going to Fenway Park with my son is anything but an opportunity to pass the time away. We share the time together fully present in the moment, cheering, goofing around with the fans around us, talking about the intricacies of the strategy, and singing "Sweet Caroline."

We give the gift of time to others. That gift of time must be cared for. A presenter who runs long and uses more time on an agenda than allotted is acting as a careless steward of the gift of time. The elevator pitch is really an exercise in taking some time from someone whose attention we desire. If we take too much, we fail. Successful time management when sharing your own story is not magic. It's a learned skill that can be practiced and mastered.

At work I led a team of geographers. The agenda for our Thursday morning staff meetings was a shared doc that all participants could add to. Each topic was owned by someone to lead and tagged with a priority. We could geek out for about 20 minutes on any given topic – Geographic Information Systems (GIS) and the mapped data supporting them were nearly 100% of our work life.

My supervisor's staff meeting, however, was a different story. He had 10 reports. Simple math tells me that GIS was about 10% of his work life. So I gave myself two minutes, and no more, to cover that same topic, because I could only expect 10% of his attention. His supervisor had about 4,000 people in his organization. My team of 30 was three quarters of 1 percent of the team. Again, using simple math I figured I could expect nine seconds of his time to share what would otherwise be a 20-minute story. Those nine seconds I treated as his gift to me (even if I stalked him by hanging around outside his office). If I was successful with my nine-second story, he might ask a question.

Eventually, he started asking for some more of my time. I was able to give him part of my two-minute version, and the gift of his time grew greater. As we begin to think of these conversations as an exchange of gifts, we can learn to manage that gift more graciously. We exchange our thoughts, our needs and, most importantly, our time. It is an ungraceful receiver of gifts who expects more than the giver has to offer.

I have found my 20-minute story is far better after forcing myself to create my two-minute version. Then, both versions are improved by the thought process needed to bring it down under 15 seconds, that sweet spot for the elevator pitch. In Rule 1 — Share your Story, we talked about the arc of the story. In 15 seconds we don't have much time to lay a foundation or develop character. We jump right to rising action and climax. The process of developing the three different versions of a story – and the practice it takes to get them right – indelibly locks the story in my memory.

This process definitely becomes easier with practice. And it comes with some cool side effects. When I am giving a talk and get a question about a related topic, I often have the already-thought out 15-second response at the ready, similar to how a comedian has bits that they string together for an act. This practice also allows me to manage time on the fly. Say I have 10 things to say in a 20-minute presentation. That's 10 two-minute stories. Then I get into a productive interaction with the participants and I am behind my planned schedule. No problem. I just substitute a couple of my two-minute topics with the 15-second version and we are back on schedule. The participants not only don't know that I changed on the fly; they helped drive what was important.

In the discussion afterward, they offer me more of their precious time by asking for more of mine, through their questions. At this point I simply draw from some of the details from the original two-minute version. Over a beer afterward, there might be time for an exchange that even draws from the 20-minute version … which, incidentally, is about how long it takes me to drink a beer.

With all this in the back of my mind, and a bunch of practice under my belt, I happened to step onto an elevator with the NYS CIO. That's right – literally an elevator pitch. Knowing he had an interest in economic development, I said, "Bob, won't it be great when we make enough GIS data publicly available in New York to move the dial on the economy?"

The doors opened and I walked off – with a big smile on my face. I pictured him thinking, "That guy is crazy, and I want to know what the hell he was talking about."

(c) Nate Tys

Two weeks later, at his request we had a meeting at my office with his whole leadership team. Each of my reports got a chance to share their two-minute story about the importance of the programs they run and the impact these data programs have on the people and economy of New York. Those conversations did some very positive things. No longer did I have three quarters of a percent of the executive's attention. We had widened that slice of the pie and enjoyed disproportionately high resources and support. Further, every member of my team knew they were seen, heard and supported by upper management. It also put to bed the notion that we should recoup costs by selling data, a strategy tried a decade earlier that greatly reduced the impact and reach of the data programs and added a huge administrative burden.

After retiring from my desk job, I took a short job helping my dear friend who owns a commercial construction business. I spent the fall and early winter of 2023 in the mountains of Maine. While managing a team building a huge eight-person chairlift, I had the pleasure of supervising a dynamo. This guy worked ferociously. A year after the project finished we still stay in touch. In one call he said, "I don't know how to talk to management. I just want everyone on the team to be in the right role and have everything they need to be productive. That includes the materials, the equipment, and the information they need to be effective. That way everyone goes home feeling good about what they did."

He went on to say, "But I don't know how to talk with management."

I said, "Hold it right there, cowboy. What you just said is exactly how to talk to management. The only thing you need is to say it, and stop, and listen."

Clearly, management will respond and maybe ask for ideas. Then they will be asking for the gift of more of his time. He can let the idea breathe; we'll learn more on that in Rule 9 — Play the Pause.

your turn...

Think beyond the elevator pitch

On the following pages, write down one thing you do and why it matters. Write down one thing you aspire to and why. Write down one thing you are proud of and why.

Now practice speaking slowly while boiling each of those statements down to 15 seconds. Get out a stopwatch and see if you can get them down to 10 seconds.

For extra practice pull out your resume and develop a 15-second story for each item on it. If you are preparing for a job interview, develop a 15-second, two-minute and 20-minute story for each item. If you can't come up with a compelling 15-second story about why something on your resume matters, maybe that item should be removed.

10 Little Rules for Sharing Your Story

10 Little Rules for Sharing Your Story

RULE 7
Understand Your Brain

Don't let me scare you off here – I am no neuroscientist; I have simply made myself aware of enough brain physiology to understand my own reactions to things. This, in turn, makes my stories more compelling. I have become more aware of when I feel creative, and when I feel defensive. I am making a conscious effort to understand what causes those emotions and feelings. As mentioned in Rule 3 — Be Scared, emotions and feelings are often referred to synonymously. Hopefully now you understand that yes, they are related, but are very different things.

Emotions are the body's observable physical reaction to stimulus. Goosebumps, elevated heart rate, spontaneous laughter and eye dilation are all emotional reactions. These emotional reactions are baked deep in our DNA and explained through anthropology. Emotions are accompanied by chemical releases in our bodies.

Feelings, on the other hand, are the mind's response, or our internal stories to explain our emotions. We can have some control over our feelings through our thoughts. This is a learnable, practicable skill. We can begin to feel the actual parts of the brain as they engage.

I mentioned earlier that I coach a youth mountain bike team. My favorite example of controlling emotions and feeling comes from this coaching. At the start line each racer is called up in order of their points total. This improves safety by getting the faster racers out front and it eliminates dangerous jockeying for position while racers are in tight proximity to each other. Before the call up, the racers wait in the area called "the pens." First, they respectfully participate in the national anthem, then they wait for their category. They might be in the pens for as long as 15 minutes. This can be the most emotional part of the race. They can experience sweaty palms, elevated heart rates, even nausea. Most of these emotional reactions have a negative impact on their performance.

I have the tremendous responsibility to coach some exceptional nationally-ranked racers. After a race that one of our phenoms won, both she and the girl who came in second went right to the first aid tent. They had both lost the ability to control their own body temperature. They both had blank stares, and there was no joy in their eyes.

As a coach, I felt a responsibility to prevent this from happening again. I did some research. My direction came from a podcast in the Finding Mastery series. An hour before the next race, I told my racer, "I have expectations for you for this race. Your parents have expectations. Every coach in the league knows your name. *And not a single bit of that matters.* All that matters is the expectations you have for *yourself.* You are in 7th grade. I hope one of your expectations is to have some fun. Maybe that is your top expectation."

"I bet your idea of fun is passing a bunch of the boys who are out in the category ahead of you, but that's up to you," I said. "When you get to the pens, all I want you to think about is three things you are grateful for. And when they say go, just go."

She came in a close second in that race, and was smiling at the end. We didn't have an opportunity to talk after her finish, but weeks later, after winning the varsity championship race as a seventh grader, she came up to me and said, "Hey coach, I had an expectation for myself for this race. I was not going to accept anything but victory."

"It turns out you are a badass," I said.

I asked if she had fun. With a big smile she said, "Yeah." This young person was mature enough to implement my instructions and gain control over her emotions and feelings. The part of the brain she activates with thoughts of gratitude is as far as it could be physically from the part of the brain that processes the fear of unmet expectations.

Our brains are incredibly complicated, yet many of their functions are not very sophisticated. For example, the brain reacts with the same neurological and chemical response when we watch a killer in a horror movie as it would if that killer were in the room. Likewise a photograph of a loved one can make us melt inside, just like a hug from them. In both cases the physical stimulus is very different, but the neuro-chemical responses are the same. It's our thoughts that can control the response.

The biggest impediment to telling our stories is fear of the opinions of others. This makes sense when we look at it from the lens of the first humans, who absolutely needed to band together to survive. They could not protect themselves from predators on their own. Being cast out from the tribe was indeed life threatening.

Fear of being outcast or publicly embarrassed is so strong because it is baked into our DNA. The modern lingo for this is "tribal shaming," and it's behind so many of our fears in modern life. We can modernize our mental software by training our minds. In Rule 3 — Be

10 Little Rules for Sharing Your Story

Scared, I told you about my simple meditation practice to train my mind to control my thoughts. I repeat a simple mantra. Inevitably, thoughts come into my mind. My practice is to acknowledge each thought and dismiss it as quickly as possible. With practice, the time it takes me to do that has shortened.

When I am done, I stand up and congratulate myself for controlling my thoughts. Now I can stand in front of a group with total confidence, knowing I can control (or at least dismiss) the thoughts that don't serve me well in the moment.

My second practice is one of self-talk. I started mountain biking in my mid-40s. There was definitely a learning curve, even though I was trained by pro riders adhering to a great curriculum. My son Colin climbed that curve along with me, but at a much faster rate.

Colin is the best mountain biker I routinely ride with. One day he told me, "You're a good mountain biker, Dad." I latched onto those words and now repeat them to myself every time I ride. Colin enjoys high credibility in that sport. Why shouldn't I believe him? He is not one to say something nice just to be nice. He says what he thinks.

When I speak those words to myself, I go out and act like a good mountain biker. Sometimes when I ride I speak to myself as a sports announcer analyzing every detail of my performance. "*A little bobble there, but what a recovery! This kid really makes things happen out there.*" So maybe it's a little silly; but it works to keep my thoughts positive, and help me celebrate recoveries.

OK, let's dive in. Buckle your seatbelt for a short journey into our brains. There are many parts of the brain that perform specific functions; I don't know much about most of them. I've studied three specific parts because of their relevance to sharing effective stories. They are the amygdala, the limbic system, and the prefrontal cortex.

(Technically, the amygdala is part of the limbic system, but for the purposes of this book we will treat it as a separate part. The amygdala has behaviors and functions that differ from the rest of the limbic system, and it deserves separate consideration.)

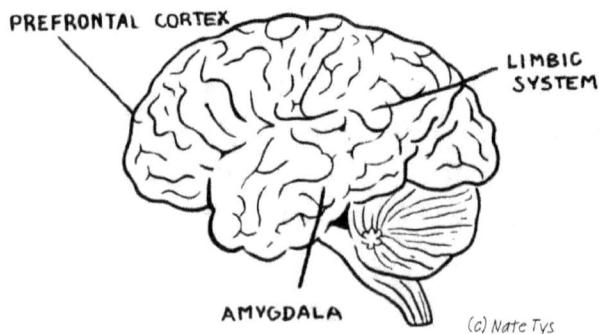

First, the amygdala. This is the part of the brain we have in common with our most primitive ancestors. An alligator's brain is primarily amygdala. In humans, it's in the back of the head right next to our spine. The amygdala fires when inputs are processed as threats. When a car pulls out into our path, this is not the time for thoughtful contemplation of the situation; it's time to slam on the breaks. The amygdala's whole purpose is to keep us alive.

You have likely heard of the fight, flight, or freeze response. These are the domains of the amygdala ... and it acts involuntarily. As I said earlier, the brain is not very sophisticated. The amygdala fires the same way in response to our senses (what we see, hear, and feel) as it does in response to our thoughts. And by default, the rest of our brain is not available to us when the amygdala is active.

In modern life, this translates into some interesting phenomena. For example, we have almost infinite opportunities to watch divisive media. Some media outlets intentionally fire our amygdala by presenting stories that are processed as a threat. They then play on our fear of being cast out of the tribe to compel us to tune in tomorrow. Yet there is good news for when we find ourselves in this cycle. The most powerful button on the TV is labeled Power.

Next, the limbic system is the part of the brain we share with puppies. You can't teach an alligator to "stay" and not eat the food you put in front of it. You can teach a puppy to behave this way by interacting with its limbic system, the more anthropologically advanced part of its brain.

The limbic system is in the center top of our heads. As in puppies, it controls our emotions and our behavior. The limbic system does not, however, control our speech, creativity, or facts and figures.

I took my son Luke on a college visit to my alma mater. He walked onto the campus and said one word: "Nope." It was his limbic system giving him that *gut feeling*. He struggled to put it into words, but something just didn't feel like a fit. So we had a nice lunch in town, drove home and crossed that one off the list.

Since the limbic system controls both our emotions and our behaviors, it is the most important part of the brain to engage when sharing your story. In his TEDx Talk "How Great Leaders Inspire Action," Simon Sinek explains that an expression of motive (or the *why*) inspires action much more effectively than an explanation of *what* or *how* (Sinek, 2010). The *why* is processed in the limbic system and gives us that gut reaction. When we understand someone's motives and find them virtuous, it moves past the amygdala and into the part of the brain that controls our non-threatened behavior.

Finally, the prefrontal cortex is the most highly developed part of the brain in humans, and it contains portions that are unique to our species. It sits behind our eyes and in our forehead. Physically it is the most distant part of the brain from the amygdala. The prefrontal cortex plays a crucial role in controlling our imagination and creativity. Along with its role in imagination and creativity, the prefrontal cortex controls our movements, personality, planning, and memory. In a study of humor, Vinod Goel, Ph.D. found increased blood flow in the prefrontal cortex of test subjects when told a joke ... even if they didn't think the joke was funny (Goel, 2001). Maybe that explains the age-old advice to start a speech with a joke. It makes sense, especially considering there is no way for us to think creatively while the amygdala and its fight/flight/freeze options are active. When the amygdala hijacks the neural pathways needed to activate the prefrontal cortex, the amygdala gains control. Fear and creativity cannot occupy the same moment.

Why does all this matter? Well, knowing a little about the regions of the brain can help us craft our stories to physically move activity from one area of the brain to another. We can control this in our own brain and even influence regional brain activation in the brains of our participants. With practice, we gain awareness of the parts of the brain as they engage. Using these concepts of brain physiology is easier than you might think. In Rule 2 — Invite Others In, I mentioned a talk I gave at the NSGIC annual meeting. The topic was data governance. This is only important because there is heated debate over the topic. I knew there could be dissenting views from the participants. I could have let the amygdala run wild and been in a threat response the whole time.

To set the right tone, and avoid the threat response, I started with this: "The next 15 minutes has the potential to be the most impactful 15 minutes of my life. But, that's up to you. I'm Frank Winters and I am happy to be here."

I paused, smiled and looked around the room. During the pause I said to myself, "I can't believe you just said that. Way to go. Let's go!"

Then I continued, out loud this time, "I approach this conversation not with certainty, but with curiosity." The talk went great and was well received. I'm not sure it will wind up as the most impactful 15 minutes of my life but, like I said, that's up to them.

What did I do there? First, by letting the participants know they have agency and are the most important factor, I got their attention, and took the pressure off myself. Then, by telling them I approach the conversation without certainly, but with curiosity, I created a psychologically safe space for both the participants and myself.

When I want to inspire action, I focus on the limbic system by talking about *why* I am thinking a certain way or *why* I am doing something. When it's time to be creative I try to activate the prefrontal cortex in myself and others. There are a few things that can help do this:

First, I shut down the amygdala by creating a safe space. I might say something like, "There are no bad ideas here." In brainstorming, I add "We haven't gone far enough if our list of ideas at the end of the session is free of truly ridiculous ideas that need to be dismissed."

Second, I might use some humor, which is also a great way to invite others into our shared experience.

Finally, I might lay out some rules to make this conversation a game. For example, before you add your thoughts to what the last person said, you must first say what you like about their idea. I also ban the words *no* and *but*. It is astounding how effective these little things are, and it shouldn't surprise us now that we know a little brain physiology.

In many of his Finding Mastery podcasts Dr. Mike states: **"The brain is the hardware. The mind is the software."**

As a person with a technical background, this really makes sense to me. As long as the hardware is working properly, has the right power, and doesn't get too hot, the software can be reprogrammed, given the right coding and inputs. The "software" of our minds can be reprogrammed, improved, strengthened, sharpened, damaged or destroyed by the inputs we give it.

Two paragraphs back I slipped in the term *neural pathways*. Signals inside our brains – and out from our brains to all of our glands, organs and muscles – are controlled by electrical impulses across synapses, the spaces between the cells of our central nervous system where electrical current causes activation (https://www.britannica.com/science/synapse). As we repeat patterns of thought or action, the individual neural pathways are strengthened, and become quicker. This is what happens when we learn the alphabet or how to pedal a bike. These pathways become repeatable and sometimes become our default patterns as the brain seeks ways to operate more efficiently.

One of the reasons that infants and toddlers need nap time is because they have not developed neurological efficiency and so expend a lot of mental energy doing and thinking in a way that is not yet routine. That is also why it's so much fun to see the world through their eyes. They have not yet developed the defaults and are discovering things in a fresh, innocent way. We can think of the neural pathways of an infant as an open field of tall grass. We can move through it, but every step is an effort. As we repeat the walk from the shed on one side of the field to the house on the other, that pathway gets worn and the trip becomes more efficient. It also becomes the path of least resistance, so deviating from it takes deliberate action and energy.

Neural pathways are shaped by everything we think and do, and become our patterns. You have heard the term *muscle memories*. Technically, muscles have no memory. They simply contract when given the electrical stimulus across the synapses. When we first learned to ride a bike, we had to think about every pedal stroke. Up and down, and up and down. Once that pathway is worn, we call it muscle memory. As a mountain bike coach, I want my riders to change the way they pedal. I want them to drop their heel as they approach the top of the stroke, then point their toe to the ground at the bottom. This engages more of their muscles and provides more consistent power. To develop an efficient pedal stroke, they need to be willing to put in the mental effort to override their default pathway and create a new one. They must diverge from the worn path through that field or muscle memory around the act of pedaling.

All of this explains why some say it's harder to teach adults than kids. I see it differently. I like to explain the pathway that we need to unwind, tell them why it matters and teach them the new skill. For example, I have a different approach teaching people to ski if they already know how to drive. To an experienced driver, the feeling of the back end sliding out is a feeling of impending doom. Yet that's exactly what a beginning skier needs to feel. Also, an experienced driver will turn their head to check their blindspot before changing lanes. Doing that on skis can put a slight rotation in the hip, causing the edge to catch. You are going down. The more we know about our own existing neural pathways and those of our participants, the more quickly and efficiently we can change, individually and as a group.

One of the most interesting things about neural pathways is we can practice them simply by thinking. I went from being an intermediate skier to an advanced skier over the summer reading and visualizing the perfect turn. Watch a World Cup racer before a competition: They have their eyes closed and they are practicing the perfect run in their mind. It is as good as (or even better than) actually skiing more practice runs.

Your stories are also rooted in your brain's pathways. I have found that some of my default stories serve me well and others don't. It's as if the good stories and the bad stories in our minds are battling. Which ones will win? The ones we feed. Simply by thinking more about what works and less about what doesn't, we begin strengthening the pathways that serve us well.

your turn...

Understand your brain

Think back to a time when you felt put on the spot or someone intentionally tried to embarrass you in front of a group. Write down how you felt.

Does this bring back a physical sensation in your body now?

Think about the setting. Who was there?
Did the person do this on purpose?
How would they be reacting to this exercise?

Check in with your body. Do you feel anything? If so, you've just recreated a threat response, with no input other than your thoughts, triggering a biochemical reaction in your body.

Now think of something you like about that person. Check in with your body again; do you notice a change?

When you engage a different part of your brain, you quiet the amygdala and create a pleasant biochemical reaction, rewarding yourself for entering the creative or empathetic part of the brain. Congratulations. You just proved to yourself that you have control over both your emotions and your feelings. You will still feel them, but you can control them with your thoughts. You can also guide your participants through that journey by employing your rules for telling your story.

Use the pages that follow to write down your thoughts.

10 Little Rules for Sharing Your Story

Frank Winters

10 Little Rules for Sharing Your Story

Frank Winters

10 Little Rules for Sharing Your Story

Frank Winters

RULE 8
Do Something Harder

I have climbed and skied the fabled runs on Tuckerman Ravine (Tux) on Mount Washington in New Hampshire every spring for 34 years in a row. I make careful study of the pitches, snow conditions and weather. On my first trip to Tux I knew I was ready; I climbed and skied a run called the Shoot. It was really scary. I met the fear with courage empowered by realistic self talk. It was a thrill.

Over the years I've connected with other experienced Tux skiers and explored far beyond the traditional runs in the ravine. One such run is called Dodge's Drop. To put it in perspective, according to the New England Ski Journal there were roughly 12.76 million skier visits in New England in the 2021-2022 season. A clear estimate of the number of skiers braving Tux each year doesn't exist, but let's say it's 10,000. That means less than one tenth of one percent of New England skiers go to Tux. Of those, I would say that less than a tenth of a percent ski Dodge's. It's no joke. It took me eight years to build up the skill and experience to say, "OK, I will ski that when the conditions are right."

(c) Nate Tys

It took another seven years to be there on a day when the conditions were right. While climbing Dodge's, the snow was untracked and perfect. The morning sun pounded down on me. There was no wind, and total silence. Then I heard music. I thought, "where is that music coming from?" I had pulled ahead from my climbing partner. I realized that the sounds I had mistaken for music were those of the blood pumping through the arteries in my neck. It sounded like the heartbeat of a baby during an ultrasound. After climbing Dodge's, it took me 20 minutes to decide to ski it. I dropped in with my heart in my throat, made the first turn, and it was ON. Somewhere between the second through 50th turn time stopped. All I remember is total focus and joy.

(c) Nate Tys

Why am I telling you all of this? It's one of my absolute favorite stories. Also, by writing this I feel that moment in my body … and even more importantly it is where I came up with the idea that if you want to do something hard, do something harder. After skiing

Dodge's, the more traditional runs on Tux like the Shoot, while still consequential, got much much easier.

Again, let's not confuse courage with recklessness. Courage is about doing something reasonable and within your safety zone while experiencing fear. Cornell Law School reports the legal definition of recklessness as, "behavior that is so careless that it is considered an extreme departure from the care a reasonable person would exercise in similar circumstances."

It is safe to say that most people should not ski Dodge's Drop, or even Tux. Likewise most people should not jump in the cockpit of a jet and try to fly it. It takes years of preparation to make either of those things reasonable. It's about the care exercised that differentiates courage from recklessness.

When skill and challenge (even consequence) are all in balance, we have a huge opportunity for growth. We also have an opportunity to achieve a flow state. In 2022, Medical News Today published this definition of flow state: "A person is in a state of flow when they are totally immersed in a task. When a person is 'in flow,' they may not notice time passing, think about why they are doing the task, or judge their efforts. Instead, they remain completely focused." (Medical News Today, 2020)

Brain Biz published an article called The Neuroscience of Flow; in it the author explains that one of the involuntary brain responses to doing something scary is the release of cortisol and adrenaline. (Brain Biz, accessed 2024). These chemicals give us the quick response and body performance needed to address a threat. They went on to say that among other chemicals released during flow state, are dopamine, popularized as the 'feel-good' chemical, and serotonin, an important mood stabilizer that helps to regulate emotions.

"Flow releases a highly potent cocktail of neurochemicals that sharpen our abilities and create optimum performance conditions," the article explains. I can tell you from experience that flow state feels really good. I cannot deliberately put myself into a state of flow. It happens subconsciously when the conditions are right. I find it interesting that I have experienced flow state more often while public speaking than doing adventure sports like ski mountaineering or mountain biking. Sometimes when I am in front of an audience sharing a story, I get this interesting sensation of being totally energized and totally calm at the same time. My brain is more completely engaged than usual, and I can think of things to say that are far better than what I think of sitting in front of my computer writing or preparing for a talk.

I believe that moments outside your comfort zone but inside your safety zone are where growth and the opportunity for flow state happens. You don't need flow state in order to grow, but it's pretty cool when it happens. While coaching youth mountain biking, I try to get all of the riders outside their comfort zone while managing risk. This does not mean I need to take them down a gnarly trail at high speed. It can be as simple as riding a series of turns through cones on a grassy hillside without using their brakes. It could be asking an experienced rider to mentor a new rider. It's pretty easy to get middle schoolers and high schoolers outside their comfort zone. Once they gain skill and confidence it can be a challenge to keep them in their safety zone. That's where coach training comes in.

My favorite example of doing something hard by doing something harder came about when asked to teach a course in our church about sexuality and relationships to 8th graders. While there was really no risk, I found that idea terrifying. Now I tell myself, "If I can talk about that to 8th graders, I can talk about anything to anyone."

your turn...

Do something harder

Think back to the hardest physical thing you have ever done. Now remember the hardest non-physical thing you have done.

What do these things have in common? Were you within a reasonable measure of safety?

On a scale from 1 to 10, with 1 being no problem at all to 10 being life threatening, what was your safety score on each?

Now think about where you were in your comfort zone. On a scale from 1 to 10, with 1 being no problem at all to 10 being totally wigged out, what was your comfort score?

How did it turn out?

How did you feel afterward?

How do you feel about those experiences now?

Given what we have covered today, if you had another crack at those situations would you do anything differently? ("No" is a perfectly acceptable answer, by the way.)

Picture something you can do in the communication realm that has little risk, but makes you really uncomfortable. Write it down on these pages.

I don't need to challenge you to go do it. I think you just challenged yourself. As I wrote in the beginning of this book, the promises we keep to ourselves are a key source of confidence.

10 Little Rules for Sharing Your Story

10 Little Rules for Sharing Your Story

10 Little Rules for Sharing Your Story

RULE 9
Play the Pause

Although my major was geography, my funded research at the University of Idaho was through the Agricultural Engineering Department. This turned out to be a blessing. Students from developing parts of the world come to Idaho to learn to irrigate in their home countries. I got close to a few of those students.

I invited my friend Mattay from Zambia to a party my housemates and I were throwing. He asked if he could bring a friend and, of course, I agreed. Well, this party was a little loud and a little rowdy. At one point I stepped out onto our back deck and found Mattay and his friend deep in a conversation, which they invited me to join. I don't remember what the conversation was about, yet more than 35 years later I still remember how it felt. It was slow, patient and thoughtful. It was a refreshing break from the pace of what was going on inside. They each patiently waited for the other to finish, paused and had something thoughtful to add. My heart rate lowered and I joined in, adjusting to their cadence. Just remembering that conversation lowers my heart rate 35 years later and puts a smile on my face.

A world away from Zambia or Moscow, Idaho is the little ski area called SkiVenture, in a small town in New York. This all-volunteer club has been in existence since 1937 and never had an employee. With support from Stio apparel company and Darn Tough socks, my friends Connor and Josey Brady spent three years making a documentary about SkiVenture. The movie is less about skiing and snowboarding and more about connecting with a group of people who share a common dream and put energy into making it come true.

Connor and Josey had finally boiled down the hours and hours of sound and video, and they shared a 14-minute draft with the media people from the sponsors. The sponsors loved it, and had one suggestion: "Let it breathe." Connor and Josey took that to heart, trimming some of the voice-over to let the images tell the story. The results were stunning; playing the pause between voice-overs gives the audience more opportunity to take in the message, and find their own meaning in it.

(Scan the QR code to watch the full length version of "Take Me to SkiVenture" on YouTube.)

These two experiences popped into my head when thinking about you and how to explain the idea of the pause. Whether learned from people from other cultures, or from film, wine, music, cooking, meditation, or scripture, we find value, insights and energy in the pause. When you open a fine bottle of red, what do you do? You let it breathe.

Think of your favorite drum riff. I bet there is power in the syncopation and the space between the strikes. My favorite drum riff is at the beginning of "Burning Down the House" by the Talking Heads. It's the pauses that get me, every time.

(c) Nate Tys

Barbecue chefs and grill masters have different opinions on almost everything. The one thing they have in common? **Let it rest.**

Pausing to put our busy minds to rest is the cornerstone of meditation practices around the world. The story of creation in Genesis 2:1-3 says that on the seventh day God rested. In Hindu teaching, Shiva and Vishnu, two important gods, are believed to practice stillness.

Early in my public speaking career, I wanted to get as many words out there as I could so I could be understood. In my haste to get words out, I added words like "um." I have grown a little since then.

Tying back to Rule 4 – Read the Room, I now put more thought into the frame of reference and feelings of the audience. With them in mind, I deliberately give them time to think. It's one thing if they enjoy or even believe my stories. It's entirely another if they take a moment to make them their own. The filler words like 'um' are hard to eliminate, but easy to replace with a deliberate pause. Nature abhors a vacuum, yet a thoughtful pause is not the same as nothing. It makes the fillers go away and can replace them with something wonderful.

During a public speaking workshop I was asked if I worry about being interrupted. The short answer I gave is that while deliberately playing the pause, I have never

10 Little Rules for Sharing Your Story

been interrupted. After letting that thought breathe, I think about the times that I have been interrupted. People who routinely interrupt I have found to be self absorbed, insecure, influenced by drugs or alcohol or any combination of those things.

At my friend's brewery I ran into a guy I had met there a few weeks earlier. The conversation came around to something that I had just written about. I said, "I just wrote an article about that..." He jumped in with, "ooh I wrote an article too" and went on to tell me about his totally unrelated article. I am pretty sure he was chemically altered and just needed to be heard. I took a sip and patiently listened. My son asked me why I spent so long talking to that guy. I said I didn't. I listened. That's what he needed. I have to admit that I am not in a rush to have another conversation with him but, while engaged, I did my best to give him what he needed.

When on stage, I often work a deliberate pause in before saying my name. That pause is just a little longer than the participants expect or are even comfortable with, and boy, does it get their attention. I have gotten over the fact that sometimes people think I'm crazy. In fact, I kind of get a kick out of it.

On a text thread just this morning, one of my three brilliant sisters apologized for sounding crazy. She got three loving responses basically saying you be you, we all celebrate our own special craziness.

Playing the pause is one of my rules for sharing my story for four reasons:

- First, it gets people's attention.

- Second, it might make people think I'm a little crazy, and crazy people are more memorable than people who hide their craziness. Actually there are two types of people in this world — those who admit they are a little crazy and those who deny or hide it.

- Third, playing the pause gives my participants time to think, and even interject. A thoughtful interjection is different in my mind than an interruption.

- Finally, there is energy in the pause. A well placed pause can raise goosebumps.

your turn...

Play the pause

Stop for 20 seconds. I mean stop everything. Think about only your breathing. If thoughts come into your mind, dismiss them.

How did you feel during that pause?

Now, think about your favorite song. Are there any pauses? Is there energy in those pauses?

Finally, think about the last talk you gave or the last story you told.

What was the most important point or part?

Did you pause to let that sink in?

Use the space on the following pages to write about the experience.

10 Little Rules for Sharing Your Story

10 Little Rules for Sharing Your Story

# RULE 10
Embrace the Joy

    As you become more adept at sharing your story, you will have increased opportunities to feel the energy from the experience. It's an elusive thing, but the interaction between you and your participants around a well crafted story can be full of palpable energy. For me that's where the joy is. I have come to expect, and actively look for, the moments of joy in storytelling. I bet it will only take a small instance of storytelling joy to plant a seed in you that will grow.

    Rule 10 was going to be Have Fun, but after listening to Dr. Mike interview Jim Nantz, the CBS Sports broadcaster, I changed it to Embrace the Joy. Jim told a story of walking into the broadcast booth and someone told him to have fun. He said something like if he were to really take that advice, he might rip his shirt off, slam a beer and do a touchdown dance. That would be fun, but highly inappropriate. Instead he finds the joy in the game and in conveying the energy of the stadium to the audience all around the world. By focusing on others, he finds joy in telling the story of the game and the people involved as the story unfolds around him.

In my younger years I put a high priority on fun; I put a lot of energy into trying to be happy. Then I started focusing more on joy. Now my goal is fulfillment. Don't get me wrong. I still get my share of fun for sure, but with my focus on fulfillment I get a deeper satisfaction. Fulfillment as a driver also allows me to put a smile on my face while doing things I otherwise wouldn't enjoy.

My dyslexia as a child was not diagnosed. Reading, writing and spelling came very hard for me. A younger me, focused on fun, could not imagine writing a book. Hell, I wasn't interested in *reading* a book. I am writing this section on a flight home after a great meeting, where I gave a talk and got lots of positive feedback. That started a few conversations about this book and my approach to public speaking. The conversations went beyond encouraging, and were joyful. I have a sense that the conversations started this week are not over. The anticipation of continuing these conversations also gives me joy.

10 Little Rules for Sharing Your Story

(c) Nate Tys

Did you ever marvel at the energy of a two-year-old? My theory is there are lots of sources of energy in our lives. One of the strongest sources of energy comes from discovery. A toddler is in a constant state of discovery.

The notion that there is energy in discovery hit me hard during my first experience around mountain bike coaching. My son, Colin, was already connected with the R-Cubed mountain bike team and wanted to race in their colors. That team, however, did not have an official presence in the National Interscholastic Cycling Association, so for his first season, Colin raced as an independent rider. He proudly wore his R-Cubed jersey, and raced like he had something to prove.

Returning for his second season, he asked if I would go to the mountain bike coach's summit to become an official coach. This would allow us to register a team. As an intermediate mountain biker, although scared, I agreed and went to the summit. We were trained by pro riders using a very well thought out curriculum. We were trained not only on new skills, but on techniques to teach them. My skills doubled just in the parking lot. I was stoked.

In my hotel room that night, I couldn't stop smiling as I stared at the ceiling. I had one of the poorest night's sleep ever, but got up full of energy still riding high on yesterday's discovery. It was so very clear to me that discovery is a powerful energy source in my life. As I began to coach others, I found that helping others while *they* get energy from *their* discovery, *I also* get energized. When someone I am coaching rails a turn for the first time, or finds a zen-like flow on a trail, I don't sleep well that night, likely because of a biochemical response to their fresh discovery.

I hope that we can together find deep joy and energy in the discovery of *your* personal rules for telling *your* stories. Maybe there will even be an opportunity to share our stories and the rules through which they shine together in person someday.

your turn...

Embrace the joy

Was there anything you thought about today that gave you energy?

How did that feel?

How can acting on that thought lead to a sense of fulfillment?

10 Little Rules for Sharing Your Story

Frank Winters

10 Little Rules for Sharing Your Story

YOUR TURN, YOUR RULES

What really matters most about storytelling are the questions we ask ourselves and the stories we tell ourselves. Our minds create a reality to make sense of things and fill in gaps. I tell the athletes I coach to be very careful of the questions they ask themselves because, given a question, the mind will answer it. If I ask myself, "Why am I so bad at this?" answers will come. Simply changing the question to, "How can I get better?" or "What can I try?" activates a whole different set of neural pathways in an attempt to find an answer.

You have gotten this far in the book, and we may have saved the best for last. As you develop your own rules for sharing your story, take some time and apply them to yourself. Use your name in the third person (silently or alone if you're concerned people will think you're nutty). This will break Solomon's paradox, which is failing to implement in our own life the sage advice we give others.

Telling ourselves our story in the third person puts us outside our own head, where we are often too close to see clearly. It also engages different parts of our brains (maybe that will be the subject of another book). It's pretty fun for me to think about myself as the audience when I:

1 – Share my story

2 – Invite others in

3 – Allow myself to be scared (or experience any emotion that comes along)

4 – Read the room (self)

5 – Compliment myself

6 – Think beyond the elevator pitch (boil down the essence of what makes me, me)

7 – Understand how my brain is functioning as I move through my day

8 – Challenge myself to do something harder

9 – Play the pause

10 - Embrace the joy

Following my 10 rules while sharing a story with myself, I gain perspective and clarity, am kinder to myself, accept and embrace feelings, and increase my curiosity and hopefully my positive impact on the worlds – the one in my head and the one outside. I hope that your rules for sharing your story with yourself have similar impacts.

I challenge you to carve out some time and share your story with others and with yourself. I invite you to tell me about what happened. I would love to hear your story.

Please reach out via LinkedIn at https://www.linkedin.com/in/frank-winters-gio/, or scan the QR code to connect. I would love to hear from you.

Frank Winters

your turn, your rules...

10 Little Rules for Sharing Your Story

Frank Winters

10 Little Rules for Sharing Your Story

10 Little Rules for Sharing Your Story

Frank Winters

… Little Rules for Sharing Your Story

10 Little Rules for Sharing Your Story

References

Gervais, Michael. Finding Mastery. https://findingmastery.com/podcasts

Winchester, Simon. (2023). Knowing what We Know. Barnhill Press Ltd.

Kluger, Jeffrey. (2017). How Telling Stories Makes Us Human: It's a Key to Evolution. Time.

Roll, Richard. (2022). A Tribute to Hilaree Nelson | Re-release of 364 | Rich Roll Podcasts. YouTube. https://www.youtube.com/watch?v=hIec2i7jDFA

Gervais, Michael. (2023). The First Rule of Mastery: Stop Worrying about What People Think of You. Harvard Business Review.

Pearson, Carol. (2016). 10 Little Rules for a Blissy Life. Little Rules Publishing.

Beach, Micki. (2020). 10 Little Rules for Finding Your Truth. Little Rules Publishing.

Raman, Aneesh and Flynn, Maria. (2024) When Your Technical Skills are Eclipsed, Your Humanity Will Matter More than Ever. New York Times.

Sinek, Simon. (2010) How Great Leaders Inspire Action. Ted.com
https://www.ted.com/talks/simon_sinek_how_great_leaders_inspire_action

Goel, Vinod. (2001) The Functional Anatomy of Humor: Segregating Cognitive and Affective Components. Nature Neuroscience, 4(3):237-8.

Medical News Today. (2020). What a Flow State is and How to Achieve It.
https://www.medicalnewstoday.com/articles/flow-state.

Brain Biz. (accessed 2024). The Neuroscience of Flow.
https://brainbiz.com.au/the-neuroscience-of-flow/

**Stay connected to the
10 Little Rules community
@10littlerules**

10 Little Rules for a Blissy Life
by Carol Pearson
10 Little Rules for Your Creative Soul
by Rita Long
10 Little Rules of Hank
by Wendy Price
10 Little Rules for Finding Your Truth
by Micki Beach
10 Little Rules for Mermaids
by Amy Hege Atwell
10 Little Rules for the Modern Southern Belle
by Beverly Ingle
10 Little Rules for Serving You
by Amy Hege Atwell
10 Little Rules for Sharing Your Story
by Frank Winters
10 Little Rules When Good Jobs Go Bad
by Kathleen Goggin

Watch for more 10 Little Rules books
launching soon at
www.10littlerules.com

www.ingramcontent.com/pod-product-compliance
Lightning Source LLC
Chambersburg PA
CBHW050331010526
44119CB00004B/127